AS THE WORLD BURNS

The Sonnets of George W. Bush

**and other poems
of the 43rd presidency**

AS THE WORLD BURNS
The Sonnets of George W. Bush

**and other poems
of the 43rd presidency**

Ken Waldman

Ridgeway Press
Roseville, Michigan

Cover Design: Stephen Bright
Book Design: Able Josiah

Ridgeway Press
P.O. Box 120
Roseville, Michigan 48066

1 2 3 4 5 6 7 8 9 10

Acknowledgments:
Folks who have helped out a lot: Bryce Milligan, John Crawford,
David Baratier, Tom Hunley, Kamala Platt, Jan Boney, Scott Pearce,
Tory Russell, Jim and Martha Stey, David McCormick, Russell Braen
and Alane Hartley, Ms. Mars, Michael Woods, Dan Henry, Jordan
Wankoff, Pam Miller, Pat Fitzgerald and Robin Dale Ford.

Contents

Jon Stewart on the Rumor of His Campaign for the Presidency of the United States

Yes, it's been reported I've been, how shall
I say, *recruited* by the Democrats
for '08. *Oh my god*, I tell you that's
absurd. (*Absurd* our TV word for *full
of bullbleep*). A serious campaign calls
for money you and I don't have. That's what
finance reform is said to be about.
(Me, I can't even afford a wee small
team of advisors, consultants, handlers—
though maybe I could just let Comedy
Central, uh, staff the war room; except there's
proof they're already doing just that. Really,
how else to explain Bush, Rumsfeld, Cheney.
Their antics are *always so damn crazy*.)

I

George W. Bush: On Privacy

I don't understand why the discussion
continues. It's not about government
overstepping bounds. It's the president
fulfilling his sworn duty: protection
for the entire U.S. population.
No, it doesn't matter how much we've spent
if we need to spend more. Look, I'm against
wiretapping neighbors. I'm for a nation
that is safe and secure. And we're a great
nation. Always have been. Always will be.
And what that means is we cannot wait
for the insurgents to enter. Privacy?
We cannot have people keeping secrets.
Freedom demands sacrifice. Let's not forget.

George W. Bush: On God

I feel the supreme being inside me.
I know he's there guiding me to do what
I must. He sure is powerful, no doubt
about it. He lets me be totally free,
but I willingly submit. Serenity,
security, prosperity are what
I own. I need nothing more. I just put
my life in His hands. He's blessed this country,
which is most important. He's the master.
To a man, we're awfully weak. With God
we can do anything. How I love Him,
a deep love that grows. To fight disaster,
I listen to Him, and learn. I love God—
God who loves both the brilliant and the dim.

George W. Bush: On Friendship

I have friends because I'm a friendly guy.
You know, like a friendly next-door neighbor,
who you might have over New Year's, Labor
Day, July 4th. It's fine being friendly—
I like it, am good at it, and do try
to reward my friends. Read any paper
and they throw dirt on what's truly proper—
a friendly guy doing hospitality
in a West Texas way. I have the best
friends in the world. They're leaders of countries,
industries, ball teams. My friends pass the test
because we share concerns. It's a pity
everyone isn't my friend. I want to be
friends with everyone. I want loyalty.

George W. Bush: On Sobriety

I'll admit I was once a wild stallion
who liked to sow oats. Okay, sure, I learned
from the experience. I must have burned
a few brain cells at parties. Not a million,
but not far off. A lot. There are billions
of things I might have become. But I turned
myself around, let my heart soar, and earned
this life. Now I follow no opinion
but my own. I won't mince words here. Quitting
was hard. It was hard staying home, sitting
without the lights, the live music, the booze.
But I had nothing to lose. No excuse.
Days passed. At last a vision. I would serve
God, family, my country. I got nerve.

George W. Bush: On Inarticulateness

Look, I know I'm not your English teacher.
Sometimes the words don't come out as I mean.
This language—it's a big problem that's been
with me my whole life. A public speaker,
I can't be shy. Just like a good preacher
forges on, me too. Maybe it's my genes—
all my weaknesses, and strengths. At eighteen,
starting Yale, I may have been a dreamer,
but I'd never dreamed of this. Still I took
debate, read a few books, graduated
with my class. God must have had his own plan.
He made me a simple, plain talker. Look,
people relate. They vote. It's such a great
great thing. Their president as common man.

George W. Bush: On ANWR

The Arctic National Wildlife Refuge.
Certainly that's one place we ought to drill.
We need oil and experts say it'll spill
out the tundra there. This is something huge
inside our lands. No Middle East excuse
to hold us hostages. It makes me ill
when I hear it's fifty-five bucks to fill
a tank. I've been elected twice to choose
the country's direction and no one wants
these high gas prices. This affects us all.
It's a simple issue. Let me be blunt.
Drilling is essential. We need more oil.
This wasteland is reserved for me and you,
not just for—what are they called?—caribou?

George W. Bush: On Iraq

There's nothing to say but what's been said.
We're winning. Everyday shows more progress.
We're moving to a position of less
troops. The insurgency is almost dead.
There's democracy—an elected head
of state. Saddam's out. No one has to guess
the ultimate outcome. It's been tough, yes.
Very, very tough. I tell you I've prayed
a great deal for our brave men and women,
and I've been distressed at the loss of life.
This effort has shown true American
grit. We're making the world safer. My wife,
Laura, thanks me every night for having
the courage. No, we will not be leaving.

George W. Bush: On Criticism

Let me explain. I hear it and I don't.
I won't let negativity affect
what I have to do. I've been elected
twice, which is quite a testament. I won't
let my country down. On the big phone-in
radio shows, there's still no disconnect—
most folks support me. But when you dissect
TV, papers, and magazines, you can't
help but see the liberal media
in action. They're so lacking real ideas
that they tear down whatever's in place. We're
governing a world that fully knows fear.
September 11th threatened us all.
Steadfast in my beliefs, I *will* stand tall.

George W. Bush: On *The New York Times*

The prime paper of liberal bias,
their writers can make any story slant.
I haven't read it for years. I can't
stand negativity. They're a virus
and plague. Yet they believe they're more pious
than the rest of us, doing what they want,
breaking events they judge most important.
Their agenda, though: anarchy, chaos.
Give me the *Washington Times* any day.
There, at least, I can browse a few minutes,
take in what I need. I always do stay
current despite media spin on it.
The New York Times, as news source, is useless.
It's my business how I run my office.

George W. Bush: On Daydreaming About Music

It was either Willie Nelson or Townes
Van Zandt, and I felt right at home, speakers
blasting. No concerns about spies, leakers,
anything with my job. No Michael Browns.
Nothing of Seymour Hersh. Not one of the clowns
I've long endured—the liars, the cheaters.
As the president, I've had to answer
to everyone. And, yes, I've stood my ground.
It helps to go to that place with headphones—
guitar, bass, drums, maybe sax, a trumpet,
some swing fiddle. Of course the pedal steel.
In crowds I might pretend to be alone
with Johnny Gimble or Lyle Lovett.
Something loud with twangy blues. Something real.

George W. Bush: On His Visionary Dream

The noon sun shone like a giant round sword.
I grew euphoric when I saw the blood
that drenched the sky. The red wetness felt good
like my heart had just been opened. The Lord
is my Shepherd and I was flying toward
His House. I knew there was plenty of food
awaiting me. I was starving. My mood,
I said, euphoric. There's no other word
to explain this. The brightness, the colors,
the feelings, the hunger. I was soaring.
In my head I could see all the others
equally high beside me. Majoring
in God, I heard a chorus sing. The sound
stirred me. In tears, I was wearing a crown.

George W. Bush: On His Second Dream

Letters rose: *i, e, o.* The names: Spiro
Agnew, Dan Quayle, Richard Nixon. I saw
my dad's name too. And mine. Then I saw
Abe Lincoln. And Jesus Christ. The heroes
of history. I saw a few zeroes
too. Large round O's. Goose eggs. Nothing at all,
but a string of circular ovals tall
as Texas. And then I saw old Nero
fiddling away. I thought big frat party—
a white toga-clad man making music,
a bit too loud maybe, but certainly
in tune. The fiddle was lost to flames next.
Fire and smoke. I stood before a mirror,
and saw America's first emperor.

George W. Bush: On His Relationship with Karl Rove

Me and Karl go back. Thirty-some years back
before I even got in politics.
There were problems. And Karl was there to fix
them good. He knows people. Knows all the facts.
Never forgets a thing. Knows what a tax
cut can do. Isn't afraid to go mix
it up and get dirty. He's athletic
in that way, which is how we see Iraq.
Hard-fought, like the playoffs. The terrorists
are rough. I don't have the details myself,
but we meet: Karl, Dick, Don, Condi, Bill Frist,
the rest. *We're on top, George—don't get yourself
all worried* is what I hear. If Karl Rove's
whispering, I can trust. To me, that's love.

George W. Bush: On Polls

I don't follow polls. This is not about
popularity. My job is to make
this nation stronger. My goal is to make
the world safer. There's no place here for doubt.
I do what I have to, and work without
regard to opinion. For god's own sake,
a leader has got to stand up straight, take
charge, and finish what he's started. Since I'm out
in front, I'm the target. I'm strong enough
to remain firm in my beliefs. I'm tough.
My advisors tell me about numbers.
Fifty per cent, forty-five, whatever.
But the choice isn't up to the public—
it's up to me. I'll decide what I like.

II

Questions About Diebold, and the Others

What can anyone make of a CEO
who said he'd deliver an election
when his company sold the contraptions
that calculated votes? And to follow:
can a so-called democracy allow
such a boast without investigation?
Isn't this about letting scoundrels run
the country into the ground? The how-to:
lobby every state to buy computers
designed to not leave any paper trail;
permit a few Republican hackers
access. It's no trick to make numbers fail
if you know codes. To win office, take note:
it's not about voters—it's who counts votes.

Vice President, Dick Cheney

As head of a search committee, he chose
himself, which should have clued us to the long
dark eight years to come. Reliably wrong
on everything from energy to clothes,
he's the Casper, Wyoming, boy who rose
to tough D.C. insider. Being strong
has meant being brusque, rude, a jerk among
jerks. You'd like to think it's just a sly pose—
how to reconcile western frontier core,
Halliburton ties. With sinister spin,
wearing cowboy boots, he urged us to war.
The saltiest hawk, he's our hefty elf
with heart condition and boozy refrain:
Go fuck yourself, senator. Fuck yourself.

His M.B.A.

Undergrad at Yale, master's from Harvard,
you'd guess most superior business sense,
or at least intellect. In this instance,
guess again. Though his wallet's single card
reads *U.S. President*, we've also heard
of past jobs, serial mismanagement,
the utter follies of dollars and cents,
bankruptcies and worse. I wouldn't buy lard
from a quickshop he worked, yet there he sits
lording over nine far-reaching planets,
moving armies like tokens on a board.
If only he'd spend what we could afford.
The M.B.A. is a con man's degree—
snake oil without English and History.

Condoleezza

Our no-nonsense secretary of state
could have come from pulp fiction. Stanford prof
hand-picked to help run the show, she's smart, tough,
black, with hair hard as a helmet. Lifts weights.
A dark gaze that will pierce, and penetrate.
Don't mess here, it says, *because I play rough.*
Loves football, classical music, men buff
as her (but there's never time to flirt). Fate
drove her west to Denver, Palo Alto,
east to D.C. where she circles the world
for the U.S.A. How much does she know?
Enough to have known how it would all unfurl.
Alas, our gal Condi's no paperback
heroine. She, too, was in on Iraq.

Sonnet with 15-Lines for George W. Bush

Soon, the number of Americans dead
in Iraq will surpass the number killed
on 9/11. And the grand total
of Iraqis critically wounded
or dead—twenty times that. I've wondered
why no one talks about this: that we're all
countrymen when it's innocent people
lost to violence. The president said
war was necessary: he had proof
Iraq owned weapons of mass destruction.
I heard no retraction after that goof,
not even sorry-for-the-invasion
(only torturous justifications).
Mr. Bush just acted in character.
He's born to a line of war profiteers.

The Wife

His great asset, Laura, the first lady,
reluctant campaigner, intelligent,
attractive, classy, soft. She's the silent
partner, former librarian, steady
advocate for literacy. One theory:
how awful can this fumbling president
be if he's married to her. What she's meant:
credibility. She seems so friendly,
happy, wouldn't abide her husband's worst
policies, would she. You'd think she'd say *George,*
honey, our millionaires don't have to be
billionaires—let's help the others. The first
lady, though, is foremost the wife. She's a scourge,
like him. She enables. She's as guilty.

Abu Ghraib

What could have been more incriminating?
Photos of naked men flanked by snarling
dogs. Blindfolded Iraqi underlings,
hands protecting genitalia, waiting
for the guards to finish the debating
and get on with the session. Breathtaking
to imagine. And what about the egging
of the culture, the forced masturbating,
other big indignities we can't yet
document? Someone with a camera let
click that one first shot, capture a moment.
We're liberators, says the president,
ignoring the disconnect. *We're guilty*,
I say, *of humiliating a species.*

The Mother

No one ever wanted to address her:
tart, regal, cold-blooded, imperious.
As a girl, she stormed outside furious
if she didn't get her way. Much later,
a tall teen, no great physical allure,
she took to money, breeding, curious
ambitious young men who were serious
about prospects. She married one, wealthier
than she'd hoped even. She gave him boys.
Dutiful wife, the indispensable
partner, his top confidante to the joys
and horrors of power. Impossible
to imagine her in bed, intimate.
Her true love: George W., the infant.

Military Man

What's worse: going AWOL from his one post
as a pilot; allowing his rival,
a true combat hero, to be smeared all
summer by that Swift Boat crew; to have lost
support not only of the country, but most
of the army—so even generals
spoke harshly; to have been responsible
for the plight of Iraq—the monstrous costs
in human life, world peace, U.S. dollars.
Neutral observers agree that the war
has worsened under the long occupation.
As commander, he's a failure. We're in
this tight spot because a rank amateur,
a dilettante, is chief. Now that's terror.

Donald Rumsfeld, Secretary of Defense

A two-bit player in the November
2000 hijacking and coup, he rose
as phoenix post-9/11, proposed
a streamlined war, civilian defender
of the corporate state. They all wondered
when he'd be let go, the dinosaur, most
arrogant bastard. His powerful foes:
retired four-star generals and other
big names within the administration
and out. With Abu Ghraib, further losses
in Iraq, the sheer numbing magnitude
of the charges of incompetence in
his control, you'd think his embattled boss
would act. But all we hear: *No worries, dude.*

Vietraq

Someday we'll see a movie, Vietraq,
with Bill Murray as George W. Bush.
There won't be much soul-searching but for Rush
Limbaugh, in a cameo, snorting crack
while ruminating how he'd gone back
on drugs. Mainly it'll be about the push
to war, the shock and awe, the great big crush
of troops, Baghdad falling, and then the lack
of cohesive post-invasion planning.
So much sheer lunacy. So much bloodshed.
A few Vietnam shots of men landing
in hospitals, missing arms or legs. Head
wounds too. Then Iraq footage. Bill Murray
plays it puzzled, lost, in no great hurry.

III

George W. Bush: On Patriotism

There are enemies within our borders:
the doubters, the skeptics, the naysayers.
Media criticism is so unfair.
I'm fighting the liberal elite here.
They say they're Americans. Instead they smear
our troops. Americans? I say compare
those false prophets to real freedom-lovers
who understand the true source of power.
Patriotism is not a sometime
pursuit. It means blessing God for this land
of riches. Anything less is a crime.
I tell you it's so difficult to stand
silent when I see countrymen disagree.
That's why we'll fix the judiciary.

George W. Bush: On Stress

I'm sick of the media making fun
of my so-called "illogicalnesses."
I know there's no such word. Instead there's stress,
always stress. Illogicities are one
of the unfortunate situations
I face daily, or more often. The mess
of the world can't be overstated. Yes,
we're in a war for more butter and guns.
Between butter and guns, I mean. It's better
getting to choose. The insurgency
would like us to use more butter. I say
we'll never be a nation of quitters.
I believe this U.S. Presidency
has strengthened me. That's the American way.

George W. Bush: On Vacation

How I love Augusts off, back at the ranch,
the early morning cool, a long bike ride
on trails, maybe Lance Armstrong right beside.
After a long nap, I'll chainsaw branches,
stack wood, cut kindling. Once I dug a trench,
but that was when I was governor. I'd
love to dig one more, say if the dog died,
but for now there's no need. Days at the ranch
fill me with purpose. The early workout,
a big breakfast, some paperwork to stay
caught up, lunch, sleep, something sweaty outdoors.
Then shower, dinner, off to bed. About
twice a week I'll fly somewhere to fundraise
or show leadership. I do get ball scores.

George W. Bush: On Debt

Personally, I don't know much about
this, though we've got tremendous experts
heading our treasury. I'm alerted
to the issue, and the rising amounts,
which is why it's on my mind. I don't doubt
this country will pull through. Debt shouldn't hurt
us a bit. We're strong people, used to dirt,
difficulties, sacrifice. Live without
if you need to. But continue to shop
and support your favorite merchants. We're
spending what we need in order to stop
terrorism. And we're succeeding here.
And if we succeed, we're safe. It's easy,
thanks in part to our allies, the Chinese.

George W. Bush: On Iraq II

Look, I never said it was to going to be
easy. *Mission Accomplished* only meant
we'd taken Baghdad. The press misrepresents
everything. With no Saddam, Iraq's free
for the first time in recent memory.
We're building new hospitals, apartments,
schools. Oil production is good. We've sent
fresh troops. We're nearing total victory.
I hear reports of a greatly weakened
insurgency despite the newspapers'
myths. I've made plans to visit one weekend
for support. I couldn't be happier.
As we fight terrorism over there,
we're safe here. I've made our borders secure.

George W. Bush: On Biking

This is what I enjoy: no one in sight
I pedal hard, the illusion that I'm
alone. It's my flat-out favorite time
on the job. Sweating, I think just how bright
our future: we can do anything. White
can be blue, or green. Pennies can be dimes
or dollars. We've won the big war on crime.
Iraq is democratic, and quiet.
I'm comforted by my guards who follow
close behind. Every citizen should feel
so secure. How I love my ranch, my days
here in Crawford. My great country allows
me to serve. But here I'm on my seat, wheels
spinning, a rugged trail. All is okay.

George W. Bush: On Drugs

I've long stopped using, but by prescription,
and I sure do enjoy both the quick buzz
from the blue pill and what the red one does,
something that calms me a little. I'm done
keeping it secret. I love medicine
when it makes me feel so damn good because
that's my birthright. As a young man I was
often high—sometimes until the room spun—
on liquor and illegal substances.
Fortunately I got clean. None of that
now. Still, there are near-daily instances
where my mind's strung a bit sharp, maybe flat,
and a pill provides just the right feeling.
When I take both at once, there's no telling.

George W. Bush: On His Dream of Gold

Somehow it felt like Jonah and the whale,
how I was swallowed down a long dark throat,
then landed by gold. I loaded a boat
with fifty or sixty bags, and set sail
for Mexico. I'd been told this was mail
I was carrying. North, we seemed to float
north, even though Mexico was south. Moat,
we passed one moat, another. Rain, then hail,
then one big blast of wind. I had no map,
no crew, no food. Only the bags of gold.
Mexico, too. I even wore a cap
that said Mexico. *It's mail*, I'd been told
by someone. Who, I had no idea. God
was nowhere. Just gold. It all felt so odd.

George W. Bush: On His Dream of Babel

They were building towers, these illegal
men and women from all over the world.
A new city was rising. Boys and girls
were working too. A bright sun felt special.
There were hardly clouds. The workers were full
of energy. Their teeth were like small pearls,
but when they spoke it was water and oil.
All sorts of languages. We needed schools,
I thought then. Big new schools that taught English.
Schools with hallways. We needed more teachers,
more houses. Meanwhile, towers, gibberish,
and a new city rising. No preachers
that I could see. Just millions of people
all busy hammering. All illegals.

George W. Bush: On the Dream of His Secret Breakdown

I dreamed of mice, nothing but all these mice
for weeks, months. Doctors medicated me,
and still the mice. How would you like to be
chased by mice? The mice were everywhere. Mice,
mice, mice, mice, mice. And then more and more mice.
Doctors prescribed stronger drugs. That's likely
how the mice vanished until there were three
gray ones left. Three little gray mice. Gray mice
with little white tails. And there was a cat,
a tomcat named Richard that liked to purr.
And there was a dog, too. A big black lab
who was old and walked funny. And a rat.
I could never forget that rat. White fur,
white tail, white whiskers. Then there was the crab.

George W. Bush: On His Dream of Saddam Hussein

In a big empty gym we were wrestling.
Really, he wasn't much competition.
I'd pinned him. No referee decision
about take-downs or escapes. There was nothing
to argue. I'd won cleanly. Carrying
the winner's trophy, I tripped. It broke in
three pieces. He came from nowhere, grabbed one,
and ran. I pursued. And we were running
up a steep, rocky mountain trail. I heard
voices try to stop us. I was gaining
on my bike now, then up flying, a bird
flapping wings. Saddam was ahead laughing.
I flew higher, faster. Full speed I soared.
Below, some Arabs exited a door.

George W. Bush: On Death

I'm no stranger. As commander-in-chief
I did not send troops to Iraq lightly.
With war there are risks. And I was mighty
sure the risks were worth it. It's our belief
Saddam Hussein meant perpetual grief
and suffering. Diplomatically
we tried to shut him down. Impolitely
he refused. He would not turn a new leaf.
We were forced. It was his high arrogance
that made him think he could fight us and win.
Saddam's crimes caused many innocents—
his countrymen, our own men and women—
to pass on. For some time we've been mourning.
God's closer then. Hard times. But heartwarming.

George W. Bush: On Faith

When you believe in God, you're never wrong.
I know that well, feel it deep in my heart.
Anyone can believe. Living apart
from God is too difficult. God is strong.
We are weak. Without God we'll go along
thinking we're fine. But once the problems start
piling, we need support. Shopping Wal-Mart
won't solve it. Nor will favorite pop songs.
I suggest church, a dialogue with God,
prayer. I know of many fine religions.
What they have in common is charity.
Go to a hospital and donate blood.
Discover your own personal mission.
Perhaps that's signing on with the army.

George W. Bush: On Global Warming

Summers it gets hot, and always has been.
Listen, we know scientists disagree
on global warming, solar energy,
and everything else. The situation
may not be what it seems. Hurricanes
happen. Hot weather happens. I don't see
climate change. I see opportunity.
A chance to start one investigation,
continue others. I propose panels,
a task force, discussion groups of all types.
We'd like input. Meanwhile we'll produce oil
as we can. For now, projects of all stripes
are underway. We need information.
My successor will make the decisions.

IV

Vice President Cheney Shoots Fellow Hunter in the Face

Label this black comedy. Here's the veep
pulling the trigger, aiming for quail, firing,
and it's his pal falling instead. I'm tiring,
finally, of chronicling each misstep
of an administration bent on some deep
peculiar need for self-sabotage. *Bring
it on*, the prez once said. That's one more thing,
as is this. Guaranteed it'll all keep
happening with our three stooges-like crew.
At least here it's grand old Republican
versus grand old Republican. I imagine
the crime scene, the need for secrecy, few
witnesses. At one point, officials even
blamed the victim, a man they called "a friend."

Post-Katrina

The ruined city didn't just happen
by accident. Despite a hurricane
that brought monster wind, tide, and heavy rain
to the Gulf, storm didn't do New Orleans
in. Built on a long, wide, shallow basin
below sea level, the spot was floodplain
between river and lake, precarious chain
of weakened links that might likely break. When
one levee failed, and that water rushed,
we saw the obvious soggy madness
that had been long imagined. City pushed
from foundation. City filled with the mess
of a deep toxic stew. Federal Aid?
While New Orleans drowned, the president prayed.

In Texas

You'd have thought with his expanding power
he might have taken a look at Texas,
set down his bike a few minutes, skipped his
nap, so he could focus home an hour
when all went crazy, the gerrymander
out of turn, that legislative train wreck
where senators fled the state for five weeks.
Surely the president could have ordered
Republican leadership to govern
by the rules in place rather than vote in
new ones that gave partisan advantage.
If not the president, who? From Orange
to Amarillo, El Paso, Brownsville,
districts changed. Mr. Bush fired up the grill.

The Courts

It shouldn't be quaint charade, the notion
each supreme court justice has earned the seat
through expertise, not politics. So it
would seem, but that's rarely how it happens.
Instead a process that's the corruption
of justice. George W.'s dad didn't
start it, tabbing Clarence Thomas, though set
new lows. That one's chief qualifications:
a black man, a judge, a conservative
so young he might serve forty years maybe.
Nothing about competency. Nothing.
Unless simply being lawyer or judge gives
one credentials to decide the country's
latest edict: George W. Bush, King.

Impeachment

Someone give Bush a blow job, the joke goes,
so we can fire his sorry cowboy ass,
this president, already ranked dead last
in history. Hard to understand those
loyalists of his. Maybe their brains froze
like busted computers. Maybe it has
to do with taxes. Maybe they like gas
at four dollars, their phones tapped. So how does
one go about bringing an impeachment?
In some cases it could start with senate
or house proceedings. Others, a lawyer
filing a suit. Here, I'd bet discontent
is so vast, we could call a strike, picket
banks, schools, Wal-Marts. Then let's see what transpires.

Conspiracy

Bookstore or library? Buy or borrow?
To stay under the radar, best use cash,
or steal. The other day, a sudden flash.
They were trailing us all day, head to toe,
bedrooms to airways, Boston to Barrow.
What we ate or taught. What was in our trash
or banks. Who were our friends. When did we wash
clothes. (The detergent, too.) The brief hello
on email or phone. What we watched last night,
or yesterday afternoon. I've learned how
librarians don't even have the right
to say the government has indeed prowled
their records, gathering data about
patrons. This is the work of patriots.

Where Yes Means No, Maybe

Finally, the slyest lawyers decide,
since it comes to this: yes means no, maybe—
depending, in part, on the policy.
Take physician-assisted suicide
and states' rights. Take the servicemen who've died
and the viewing of the caskets. The country
is gray on gray, suit against suit—so we
call in professionals who pledge to abide
by the courts, and their political logic.
No to abortion. Hell, yes, to torture.
No to privacy, or diplomatic
solutions. Where are the plain-talk lawyers
and free-thinking judges? When they're banished,
poets, then, will be the next ones vanished.

Veterans

They've come home filled with visions, missing limbs,
in caskets. I'm saying depressed, damaged,
dead. Someday we'll all have more fully judged
the era. That's after the post-mortems,
the final clean-ups, the last fatal hymns.
Our major historians will have dredged
the facts. From Saddam to the alleged
weapons of mass destruction. From war crimes
to the men and women who got broken
in Iraq. How many Americans
suffered there. And to what effect. And why.
And about the innocent Iraqis
caught in between. And then to go further
back to the source. The very first murder.

Here, Where Hitler Meets O.J.

Reduce the holocaust to pop culture.
Replace the toothbrush moustache with a smirk,
and add utter indifference to work,
a sense of supreme entitlement. Pure
100% evil, though we're not sure
the brand of megalomania. Quirky
personality: half arrogant jerk,
half one-of-the-gang. This is no John Muir
we're following. This is the little boy
lost in the woods, playing at war. This is
the callow young man who zooms across country
in his favorite red airplane. His joys?
Bike riding, brush cutting, grilling steaks. His
dream? To go down, like dad, in history.

Brother Jeb

More polished, he sits in Tallahassee,
waiting his turn. 2000 he delivered
Florida. Since then he maneuvers. Word
has it the family is not happy
George W. has made such a sorry
mess he's making every last Bush absurd—
though you could bet Jeb in '08 I'd heard
from Tampa friends who've studied the clan. Me,
I just travel around, keep eyes and ears
open. Jeb in '08? Sounds plausible
unless the elections get suspended
due to war, terror, the general fear
of a country going under. What I'll
predict: The regime will be extended.

The Daily Spin

Now there's a job, daily press conferences,
planted in front of the room with a mike,
delivering the news to the press. Like
a wall. Or a cagey electric fence.
Sly cipher who repeats the day's nonsense,
then tomorrow's same. Why not go on strike,
I wonder if reporters ever ask,
fed up with the utter lack of substance,
the chatter of their work. Why not refuse
to play fool to the joke. I imagine
the spokesperson before an empty room,
compelled to continue. Writers can choose
to fight. Here's my own humble solution:
do basic research; turn spin into poems.

V

George W. Bush: On Dad

I'm number forty-three. He's forty-one.
Sharing the experience of office
has brought us closer. I don't have to guess
the pressures he must have felt. It's no fun,
always on call, making the decisions
that affect the world. This public service
is big business. My dad understood this,
ran the country like a corporation.
He was a genius, really, not given
his due for how he transformed government,
taking Ronnie Reagan's lead, and pushing
farther. My dad was a great man, driven
by love of country. I feel I've been sent
to complete his work. It's near finishing.

George W. Bush: On Classifying
and Reclassifying Information

We cannot have people keeping secrets.
Freedom demands leadership. Let's not forget.
I don't understand why the discussion
continues. It's not about government
overstepping bounds. It's the president
fulfilling his sworn duty: protection
for the entire U.S. population.
We cannot allow another event
like 9/11. I'm fighting against
terrorists here. I'm making our nation
safer and more secure. And we're a great
nation. Always have been. Always will be.
And what that means is I'll do exactly what
I want. Haven't I explained this already?

George W. Bush: On No Child Left Behind

It works in Texas. I know in Houston,
at least in a few state-of-the-art schools.
We've reinvented policy, some tools
to help our youngsters succeed, every last one,
not just the gifted and talented sons
and daughters—but those to whom life's been cruel,
who've had bad breaks. We've had to make our schools
not only accountable, but certain
of great success. That's meant a lot more tests.
That's meant rewarding good schools, punishing
the ones that fail. We've got the very best
educational system now working.
Next task? The army has got to enlist
far more of our high-school drop-outs. They're missed.

George W. Bush: On Iraq III

I'll tell you what we've done. We got rid of
Saddam, eliminated his corrupt
regime. Yes, I know we haven't yet stopped
the violence, but we're getting close. Rough
times, but it's been worth it. You have to love
how the Iraqis have embraced reform. They topped
our estimates each election. I've watched
Sunnis, Shiites, and Kurds all vote. It's tough
to cast ballots past death threats, but they did,
and I'm proud of them. It means we're winning.
Under Saddam, conditions were squalid.
Now, everyday, they're slowly improving.
While there's no timetable for withdrawal,
history will show we made the right call.

George W. Bush: On Leakers

Sure, they have the right to say what they want.
After all, every one of us believes
in freedom. Though in the end I believe
in loyalty to our country. We can't
always just say what we want when we want
when there are consequences. We receive
countless briefings each and everyday. Leave
it to the media to twist this. Can't
they see? It's a simple thing. When people
talk about matters of security
it affects all of us. We have to take
action. The terrorists—they want to kill
people. U.S people. U.S. cities.
I fire leakers. This is the choice I make.

George W. Bush: On Jack Abramoff

No. No way. Uh uh. I don't know the guy.
So we've been in photos together two
or three times. But that's what you have to do
when you're president. You meet strangers, try
to be nice. You greet. This is one of my
duties in office. I have no idea who
these people are. No clue. I say thank-you
for coming, and then shake the next hand. Why
am I expected to know this fellow?
Because he's contributed a huge sum
of money? Because we've said quick hellos?
Because he's a loyal Republican?
I have a large country to oversee.
That's my work. I only know family.

George W. Bush: On the Environment

I'll take credit for work on clear skies
and healthy forests. That's pretty basic,
I know, but our congress passed heroic
legislation to keep our land true. Rise
and shine. Rejoice. We've got grand king-size
parklands, the biggest redwoods. All music
to me. For those who are more athletic,
you can hunt, fish, hike, bike, maybe surprise
a bear as you snowmobile down a trail.
I'm working hard at cleaning up the rest
of the country. We'll all profit from sales,
if done right. We have busy friends out west
who'll cut brush, build homes, do irrigation
to benefit future generations.

George W. Bush: On the Internet

I know people have said it's a frontier,
which should translate as opportunity.
I'm all for this electronic country
being run more profitably. It's clear
we're losing real business. We've got to steer
in a new direction. Opportunity,
that's the key word. We'll make a policy—
what's the phrase being used, two or three tiers?—
allowing some companies to charge more
to get their commercial message across.
Quicker access. That's what they'll shell out for,
the computer-users. Like toll roads. Cost
to be determined. A superhighway
of information. Like cable TV.

George W. Bush: On Health Care

It's painful to find Americans sick.
No one's to blame, but people want to be
well. And I want to help. We can agree
that someone has got to pay. We can't kick
the dying from hospitals. The poor can't pick
doctors maybe, but they're promised to see
somebody. That's the system. Charity
is working well enough. Don't get sick—
that's my first piece of advice. Ride your bike
to work, which also saves big on gas.
Take aspirin. Eat what you really like,
which makes you happy. Most illnesses pass.
Specialists and tests aren't cheap. Insurance
has risen. I know it's tough on parents.

George W. Bush: On the Twins

The girls have been good for Laura and me.
They've been quite a responsibility.
But that's true of any family.
Maybe we agree. Maybe disagree.
In the end, we respect, we honor, we
love. When the girls get in trouble, maybe
it's not "trouble" but opportunity.
That's how every good parent learns to see.
When they marry, they've been raised to marry
optimistic, patriotic young men
who'll embody values, who'll be fine dads,
who'll provide. My good daughters will carry
the next generation. I'm aging. When
my first grandson is born, I'll be glad.

George W. Bush: On D.C.

After six years, I've settled in. D.C.
isn't Crawford. But it's not Manhattan.
I can live here. I eat real Mexican,
and barbecue. The job keeps me busy—
busier than I'd like—but I stay healthy
because I enjoy Texas vacations.
Cities are hard. But this is like Austin.
And our White House staff makes it feel homey.
We've had good friends visit from El Paso,
San Antonio, Galveston. We've made
Pennsylvania Avenue more secure,
erecting walls, rerouting traffic. No
chance of car bombs. No Baghdad replayed—
we'll have no rioting here. That's for sure.

George W. Bush: On Stephen Colbert's Appearance at the 2006 National Press Club Dinner

First, he seemed funny. At least he looked good
in his tux. We'd been enjoying the night,
visiting with friends, saying hellos right
up to the keynote. Look, I never would
have guessed this pleasant-looking fellow could
ruin the mood. Whose idea, his invite?
He sure turned real nasty. Not for polite
company. It's a nice affair. Good food,
promised laughs—spoiled by a comedian
I'd never heard of, with a malicious
streak a mile wide. They say his name's Colbert.
Sounds French. At least no live television.
Whoever he was, he was a vicious
bastard. Scott, Karl, the story goes nowhere.

George W. Bush: On His Final Dream

I was a giant. Laura, too. We were so big
we crushed the roofs of houses as we walked
to buy eggs. We wanted to go home. Talked
about it almost all the time. My wig
made me look like George Washington. A pig
squealed, a tiny thing like a mouse. A squawk
from a small crow then. We were on the ark,
but in a drought. Our boat on dry land. Fig
trees. Little fig trees. Laura took my hand.
The boat rolled like a bus. Going home at last.
Farther south, we jumped out a window. Land
smelled better. Horses and sheep. Nice high grass
to our necks. Huge tomatoes. Peas and beans.
I was flea-sized. Laura, too. Life's so mean.

Other works by Ken Waldman

Poetry:
Nome Poems
(West End Press, 2000)

To Live on This Earth
(West End Press, 2002)

The Secret Visitor's Guide
(Wings Press, 2006)

And Shadow Remained
(Pavement Saw Press, 2006)

Conditions and Cures
(Steel Toe Books, 2006)

Recordings:
A Week in Eek
(Nomadic Press, 2000)

Burnt Down House
(Nomadic Press, 2001)

Music Party
(Nomadic Press, 2003)

Fiddling Poets on Parade
(Nomadic Press, 2006)

All Originals, All Traditionals
(Nomadic Press, 2006)